COLORING BOOK

Serene Little Village

The Tiny Fairies of the Flower Meadow

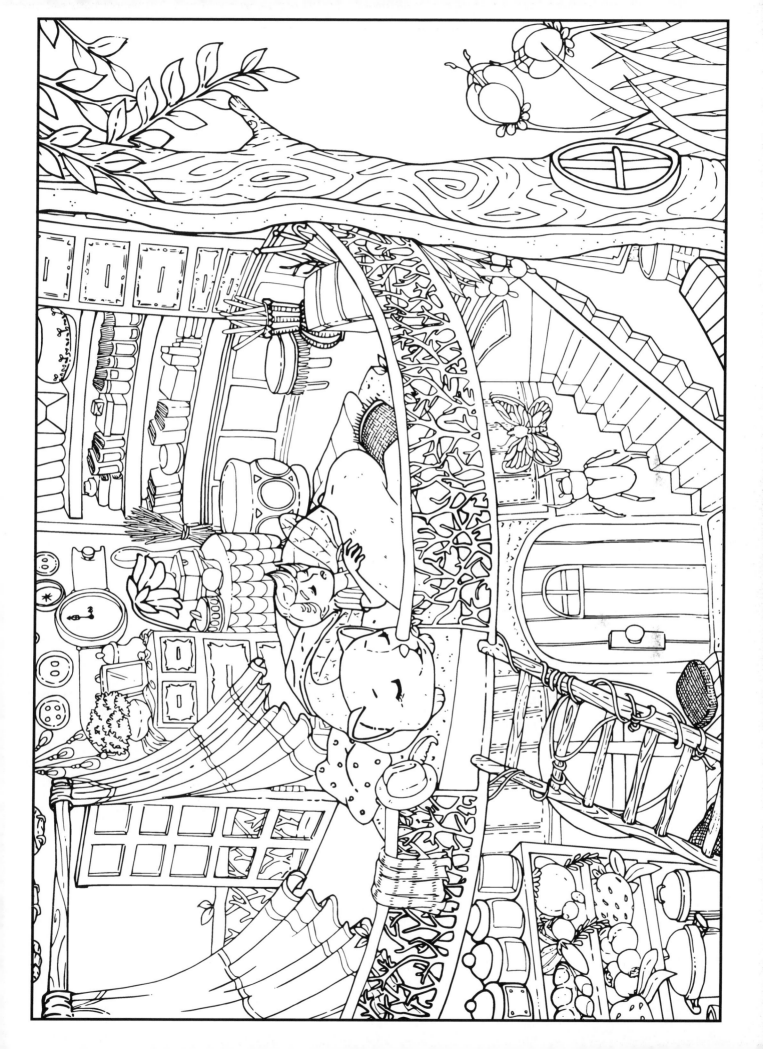

Coloring Books

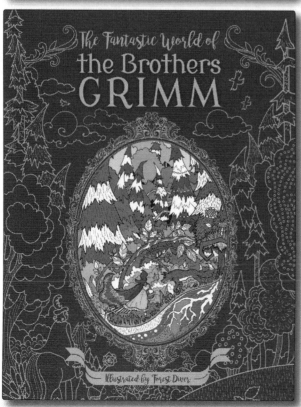

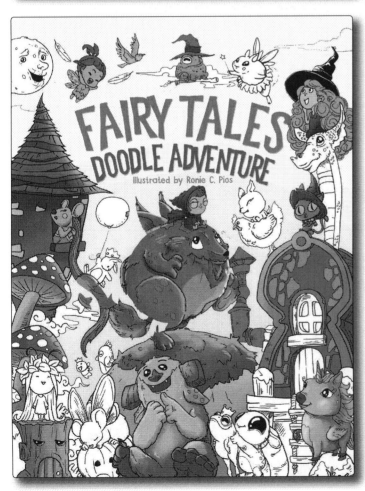

COLORING BOOK
Serene Little Village
The Wondrous Life Behind the Garden Walls

Coloring Book
KEEPERS OF THE ENCHANTED FOREST
ILLUSTRATED BY FOREST DIVER

Coloring Book
Enchanting Mermaids

Finding Wonderland
Storytroll Coloring Book

The Book of Phantastical
Dragons
Storytroll Coloring Book

Coloring Book
ENCHANTING FAIRIES

THE MANGA INVASION
COLORING BOOK
Illustrated by Boonhu

Coloring Book
Majestic Nature
Illustrated by Ilea Sivana

Coloring Book
ENCHANTING PRINCESSES,
PONIES AND UNICORNS

DINOMON
Invasion of the
Dinosaur Doodles
Illustrated by Rosa C. A.

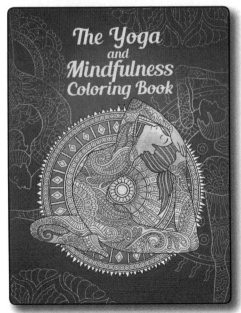

The Yoga
and
Mindfulness
Coloring Book

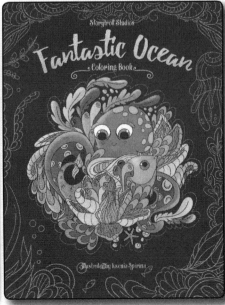

Storytroll Studios
Fantastic Ocean
Coloring Book
Illustrated by Ksenia Spirina

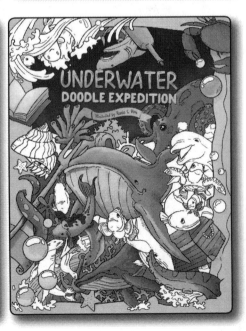

UNDERWATER
DOODLE EXPEDITION
Illustrated by Rosa C. Wu

Children's Books

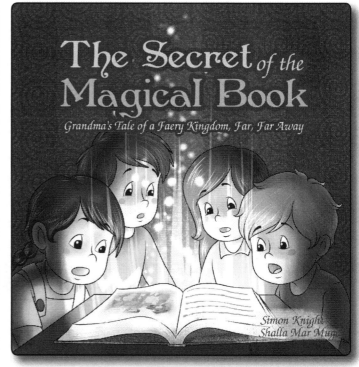

Made in the USA
Middletown, DE
12 November 2018